sacred art

sacred art

jenni davis

Publication in this form copyright © Pitkin Publishing 2005,
latest reprint 2010.

Text copyright © Pitkin Publishing

The moral right of the author has been asserted
Series editor Jenni Davis
Designed by Mark Buckingham
Pictures researched by Jenni Davis

A CIP catalogue for this book is available from the British Library.

Available through mail order. See our website, **www.pitkin-guides.com**,
for our full range of titles, or contact us for a copy of our brochure:
Pitkin Publishing,
Healey House, Dene Road, Andover, Hampshire, SP10 2AA
Sales and enquiries: 01264 409200   Fax: 01264 334110
Email: sales@thehistorypress.co.uk

Printed in Singapore

ISBN 978-1-84165-155-2   2/10

contents

introduction

Raphael's painting The Madonna of the Pinks, *in The National Gallery, London. A statuette of the Blessed Madonna and Child by Josefina de Vasconcellos (above), in Carlisle Cathedral.*

The most outstanding works of art are born out of a passion for the subject portrayed, and for this reason sacred art – arising from a deep spiritual connection with the universal source of divine love and inspiration that we know as God – counts highly among the most beautiful and powerful of all the great works. So what exactly is sacred art, and what is its purpose?

Works of sacred art are created for devotional and contemplative purposes. They are designed to connect those who look upon them with the Divine, and to unite or keep them in touch with their spiritual centre. They calm the senses and inspire the soul; telling the story of Christ's life, death and resurrection, they are both humbling and uplifting. Sacred art is challenging and intriguing, full of the extraordinary mystery of faith, and everything about it has a profound significance, from the materials used to create it to the complex symbolism portrayed within its depths.

A 12th-century stained-glass panel in York Minster. A reredos sculpture (above) in St Alban's Cathedral.

The natural and most traditional environment for sacred art is a church or cathedral; here, the paintings, sculpture and stained glass guide the viewer on a symbolic journey that echoes the Christian path of life. In medieval times, religion was central to life, and all events were attributed to God showing his pleasure – or more often his displeasure – in the actions of man. At that time, illiteracy was widespread and so presenting the Scriptures pictorially made them available to all.

Today, however, works of devotional art are also displayed in art galleries, where they are accessible to those who, in our highly literate but less spiritually focused age, are perhaps less likely to visit an ecclesiastical building. These works are wonderful treasures, which have often been rescued and lovingly restored; they are of extraordinary value not only for their important place in the history and technical development of art, but also because they give such an honest and moving insight into the beliefs and attitudes held during the period in which they were created.

Most of the works illustrated in this book can be seen in a British cathedral or art gallery; the few exceptions are included for their historic or artistic importance or simply because they are so very special.

*'Glory be to the Father
And to the Son
And to the Holy Ghost;
As it was in the beginning,
Is now and ever shall be,
World without end. Amen.'*

the artists

*M*edieval churches and cathedrals are full of remarkable images, created by skilled and dedicated – but anonymous – stonemasons and woodcarvers, glaziers and painters. Fortunately, though, we know a great deal

Rembrandt's Adoration of the Shepherds, *in the National Gallery, London. A detail (above) from* The Adoration of the Magi *by Burne-Jones in* The Hermitage, *St Petersburg, Russia.*

about some ecclesiastical artists, and to see them in their historical context is both fascinating and enlightening.

History's most influential artists, uniting the classical style of the past with the technical ability of the future, are those of the Italian Renaissance, which took place in the 14th to 16th centuries. This was a period when commercial growth led to great riches, yet religion, not materialism, was still dominant. Many of the sacred works that hang in our galleries were painted by Renaissance artists working under the patronage of wealthy families such as the Medici of Florence. Some were commissioned as church altarpieces, but in homes bedheads, door panels and even sofa backs were often painted with religious scenes. Small, hand-held panels were created as a focus for individual contemplation.

The Renaissance legacy lingers on, but today's artists mostly embrace the modern need for a spiritual connection to the work that is simpler and more immediate. Here we look at a few of the great names in sacred art.

fra filippo lippi and botticelli

Botticelli's painting The Mystical Nativity, *in The National Gallery, London. An example of Fra Filippo Lippi's* The Madonna and Child *(above), in The National Gallery of Art, Washington, USA.*

Fra Filippo Lippi (*c.*1406–69) joined a Carmelite monastery as an orphan and later trained as a painter. Unlike the many artists whose works are both sacred and secular, Lippi painted only religious subjects; but his story is not as straightforward as one might expect from his devout background. The model for many of his beautiful, gentle Madonnas was believed to be a novice nun, Lucrezia Buti; scandalously, she became his mistress and bore a child, Filippino, who also became a painter. In spite of this breach of morality, the talented Lippi was a favourite of the great Florentine families.

An outstanding feature of Lippi's work is his attention to detail, such as the folds in fabric, and he loved including very delicate, transparent haloes and touches of fine gauze. He depicts the Christ Child realistically wriggling on his mother's lap.

Lippi's light hand is also seen in the works of his pupil, Sandro Botticelli (1444/5–1510), who portrayed the grace and elegance of ideal female beauty with an equal enthusiasm.

Botticelli's works reveal much about spiritual influence upon 15th-century Florentine life – his images of the Adoration of the Magi, for example, mirror the colourful processions of certain wealthy citizens that were held every five years on Epiphany, the Magi's feast day.

Later paintings reflect the underlying fearful mood of the close of the century, when the end of the world was anticipated and the rich threw their possessions on a 'bonfire of the vanities' in the hope of last-minute redemption. *The Mystical Nativity*, painted *c.*1500, holds a tension that goes beyond joy into a fervent hope that good will overcome evil.

michelangelo and leonardo da vinci

Michelangelo (1475–1564) was a most intriguing character, deeply tormented through most of his life by a passion for the beauty and sensuality of classical style that left him feeling sinful and at odds with his innate Christian faith. He was aged over 70 when he finally surrendered himself completely to his belief in God; this makes it all the more remarkable that there is such great tenderness and spiritual understanding in the *pietà* he sculpted for St Peter's in Rome when he was only 24.

Michelangelo's most famous work is the fresco on the ceiling of the Vatican's Sistine Chapel, a project he embarked upon with bad grace since he much preferred sculpture to painting.

Leonardo da Vinci (1452–1519) was characterized by his extraordinary range of talents – a painter, sculptor, architect, scientist and engineer, he was the quintessential Renaissance man, a philospher far ahead of his time. Unlike Michelangelo, Leonardo was more than comfortable with expressing reality; his studies of nature, and in particular the effects of light and shade, are reflected in his work, which greatly influenced future artists.

Leonardo's painting *The Last Supper* on the refectory wall of the convent of Santa Maria delle Grazie in Milan is seen as the masterpiece of his religious works, albeit a sadly deteriorated one owing to over-zealous restoration.

crivelli and raphael

Carlo Crivelli's painting The Annunciation with Saint Emidius *(right) and Raphael's* The Aldobrandini Madonna *(above), both in The National Gallery, London.*

Carlo Crivelli (1430–95) was a painter of the Venetian school, and his style combines a lingering Gothic opulence with Renaissance freshness. His works are almost overpowering at first glance, so rich are they in detail; but a long, slow look reveals some interesting, sometimes even amusing, touches and a deep adherence to the principles of Christian symbolism.

Acknowledgement of the patronage of the Renaissance artists was often a feature of their works; in Crivelli's 1486 painting of the Annunciation, for example, the Angel Gabriel is – very unusually – accompanied on his visit to the Virgin by Saint Emidius, the patron saint of the town for which the altarpiece was created.

The works of Raphael (1483–1520), created during the High Renaissance period, are in total contrast. Shaking off the overly pious, sentimental style

that he had been taught by his master, Perugino, Raphael brought together the authentic composition of Leonardo da Vinci and the powerful energy of Michelangelo, then added his own elements of grace and clarity to create a unique combination of form, depth, colour and expression. The detail – for example, the soft glow he creates on the cheeks of the Virgin – is extraordinary, but so too is the simplicity, making small devotional pieces, such as the joyful *Madonna of the Pinks*, very accessible to spiritual connection.

'… those who possess such gifts as Raphael are not mere men, but rather mortal gods …'

Giorgio Vasari, 1568

dürer and rembrandt

Rembrandt's depiction of The Holy Family, *at The Hermitage in St Petersburg, Russia. Dürer's* Madonna and Child *(above), in the Graphische Sammlung Albertina, Vienna, Austria.*

A feature that gradually emerged in Renaissance painting was the depiction of the natural world as a background to the main subject, as the classical niche gave way to settings of pretty gardens and verdant countryside.

The symbolism of a garden filled with spring flowers was especially associated with the Blessed Virgin, as the Annunciation was said to have taken place during this season, and no one portrayed this imagery more beautifully than the German artist Albrecht Dürer (1471–1528).

Many of Dürer's religious works were woodcuts and copperplates; for these, and for his paintings, he spent endless hours making studies of the landscape and of natural phenomena such as sunsets. His use of ink and watercolour on paper for works such as *The Virgin with the Animals* produced an ethereal, dream-like quality.

An outstanding artist of the early post-Renaissance period is the Dutch painter Rembrandt Harmensz van Rijn (1606–69). His religious paintings form only a small part of his prolific output, but they are remarkable for the way the subjects emerge from a gloomy, shadowy background as if struck by heavenly light.

The Holy Family, painted *c.*1645, is a delightful representation of the human and divine natures of Christ. The infant Jesus sleeps peacefully in his cradle, while the Virgin watches over him, a book lying open on her lap, her face suffused with maternal tenderness. Both are bathed in a pool of soft golden light; In the shadows behind Joseph is busy working at his carpentry, while above them naked angels hover in their own shaft of divine light, showing that this is no ordinary domestic scene.

burne-jones

Detail of The First Day of Creation, *one of six Angels of Creation designed by Burne-Jones, on display at Harvard University Art Museums, USA.* The Annunciation *(above), also known as* The Flower of God, *is in the Christie's collection, London.*

The early Renaissance artists greatly inspired a 19th-century Englishman, Edward Burne-Jones (1833–98), who abandoned his theological studies at Oxford and chose instead to express his spiritual nature through art. This change of direction resulted in a wonderful legacy of sacred works in the form of paintings, stained-glass windows and tapestries.

Burne-Jones was introduced to his 'life of art' by the Victorian Pre-Raphaelite Brotherhood, a group of young artists who emulated the style of the early Italian painters (that is, pre-Raphael). An example of Burne-Jones's earliest works, *The Annunciation*, is typical of this period – it shows the kneeling Virgin bathed in divine light shining down from the Angel Gabriel, who holds a symbolic stem of lily flowers. This painting was slated by art critics for its blatant medievalism; later works, however, were readily admired for being finished 'with the utmost conscience and care'.

Burne-Jones certainly caught the meticulous attention to detail and truth to nature of the Italian artists – every leaf he paints, every feather in an angel's wing is perfect, and a gentle, respectful beauty pervades his work.

'I mean by a picture, a beautiful romantic dream … in a land that no one can define or remember, only desire – and the forms divinely beautiful.'

Edward Burne-Jones

craigie aitchison

Craigie Aitchison's 1987 Crucifixion, in the Tate Gallery, London, and (above) the 1959 Crucifixion.

As a young man, Craigie Aitchison (b.1926) began studying for the Bar, but – like Burne-Jones – soon decided that his talents lay elsewhere and changed to studying art instead. It was a negative criticism, casually made by a passing tutor, about a copy of a Crucifixion painting on which Aitchison was working, that led, perversely, to his great fascination with painting this subject, now the focus of almost all his religious works.

Upon first glance, Craigie Aitchison's Crucifixion paintings are almost childlike in nature, seemingly made up only of geometric blocks of rich, dense colour, the Cross and Christ (who, more often than not, is portrayed without arms – Aitchison reasons that everyone knows who He is, so He doesn't need arms). Then you notice the subtle gleam around the head and the incredible luminosity of the body,

portraying the light of God shining within Christ, and begin to understand that Aitchison's works are a simple, unsentimental but deeply moving focus of spiritual contemplation.

In one of his early depictions of the Crucifixion, painted in 1959, Aitchison included witnesses to the Passion in the form of angels that resembled glowing, darting insects; more recently, the witness has often been a large, ungainly dog, loosely modelled on the artist's Bedlington terrier, which gazes with a touching, unwavering attention upon the solitary, radiant figure of Christ on the Cross.

There are occasional variations to the basic formula; *Crucifixion, 1988–89*, for example, portrays Christ lit by a beam of divine light shining from above, while *Crucifixion, 2001* has a dove, the symbolic representation of the Holy Spirit, hovering above the Cross.

sergei fyodorov

Fyodorov's fresco of the Baptism of Christ, in Rochester Cathedral. An icon of Our Lady of the Sign (right) in Portsmouth Cathedral.

While most modern artists have brought their devotional works very firmly into the 'here and now', Sergei Fyodorov has opted to revive a very traditional art form – the icon.

Fyodorov, born in 1959, grew up in Soviet Russia where religious worship was banned, and his first encounter with an icon was in a Moscow gallery rather than a church. He connected immediately with this most profound artistic expression of spiritual devotion; serendipity led him to one of Russia's few monasteries, where he studied icon painting, a forbidden practice.

Although an icon is essentially a sacred image of the Eastern or Orthodox Church, its value as a focus for individual prayer and devotion has been recognized by the Anglican Church and several cathedrals have commissioned icons by Fyodorov, who now lives in England.

Fyodorov has also turned his hand to painting a fresco, completed in 2004, in Rochester Cathedral. The work depicts the Baptism of Christ, and although its style is traditional, its clarity and simplicity has an indefinable sense of today and of the future, reflecting the eternity of the Christian message.

christian symbolism

*W*orks of devotional art often have what appear to be little decorative touches – a flower, an animal, a fruit; but these usually have a symbolic meaning within the Christian tradition.

Crivelli's The Madonna of the Swallows *(right) and a detail (above) of Raphael's* The Madonna of the Pinks, *both in London's National Gallery.*

Sometimes the symbols refer to the immediate subject, such as the pinks in Raphael's *The Madonna of the Pinks*, which signify divine love. As a symbol of marriage, they also depict the Virgin as both the mother and the bride of Christ. In other instances, the symbol is prophetic – in Crivelli's *The Madonna of the Swallows*, the swallow perched above the Virgin's throne is a symbol of resurrection and so a portent of how the story unfolds.

The symbolism is derived either from pre-Christian tradition, often adapted to reflect its new purpose, from legend, or from biblical stories. It is extensively used in churches and cathedrals, which in their layout symbolize the path of life toward spiritual enlightenment.

The list of symbols is endless and fascinating; it includes the Holy Family and significant events in their lives, the company of heaven such as saints and angels, flora and fauna, even colours and numbers. To appreciate their deepest significance, we must understand the mystery of the Christian faith; just a few examples are given here.

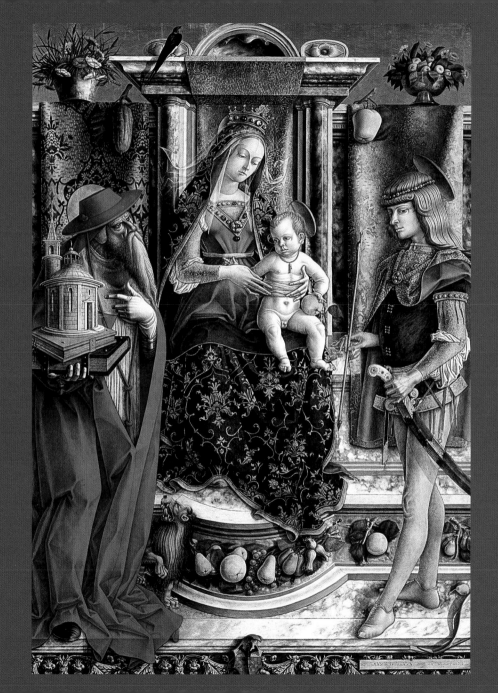

The carpet page from the St Chad Gospels, the greatest treasure in Lichfield Cathedral. A statue of the Celtic saint Aidan (below) in the grounds of the priory on Holy Island, off the Northumberland coast.

The early Christian was leaving behind what is often enigmatically called 'the old religion' of Celtic paganism. In their quest to connect with the Divine, pagans worshipped many gods and goddesses; they lived in tune with the natural world and the rhythm of the seasons, and their idols reflected this. They also observed that every living thing had characteristics that could be likened to some aspect of mankind's existence and search for spiritual enlightenment. The Christian Church

saw the value of this symbolism and adopted it to help teach their message.

The Celtic people were known to be an artistically brilliant race, and the new Celtic Christians took their ideas forward into their devotional art. The distinctive stone wheel-head 'high' crosses, erected at their sacred sites as reminders of Christ's sacrifice, are carved with Bible stories but are also decorated with designs in the graceful, abstract Celtic style, signifying the mystery of the faith. Animal and plant symbolism also appears in magnificent Celtic illuminated manuscripts such as the Lindisfarne and Lichfield Gospels.

The Renaissance artists, under the patronage of the Church, used this traditional symbolism to wonderful effect in their works. They are credited with bringing order to the mystical and spiritual meanings of the Celtic symbolic legacy.

the dove

A statue of St David with the Holy Spirit in the form of a dove on his shoulder, in St David's Cathedral. A detail (above) of the Annunciation window in the Epiphany Chapel, Winchester Cathedral.

The dove – beautiful, gentle and pure white – is the symbol of peace and of God the Holy Spirit, and makes frequent appearances in sacred art. There is always a dove in images of the Annunciation, descending on Mary as she receives the message from the Angel Gabriel. A dove also appears in depictions of the baptism of Christ and, of course, of the Holy Trinity.

Seven doves in an image represent the sanctifying gifts of the Holy Spirit: these gifts are wisdom, understanding, counsel, spiritual strength, knowledge, godliness and fear of God. Doves are often used to denote the human soul, and twelve doves in an image represent the whole of mankind.

In the biblical story of Noah's Ark, the dove flies out from the ark and returns carrying a freshly plucked olive branch in its beak, with the news that the flood-waters have receded and that God's punishment has come to an end. The combination of dove and olive branch is now recognized as the universal symbol of peace.

The dove has an affinity with several saints, including the Welsh St David – it is said that the Holy Spirit, in the form of a dove, descended to his shoulder after a reluctant but outstandingly eloquent address to a synod of bishops, and portrayals of the saint often commemorate this event.

'I saw the spirit descending from heaven like a dove, and it abode upon him.'

John 1:32 (the baptism of Christ)

eagle and pelican

A carved roof boss depicting a pelican in Chester Cathedral. A detail (above) of the eagle representing St John on the John Piper Tapestry in Chichester Cathedral. The eagle adorning the lectern in Exeter Cathedral (right).

The magnificent eagle is associated with power and the Divine. In both Christian and pagan traditions, it renews its plumage each year by flying near the sun and then plunging into water, and so is an enduring symbol of the Resurrection.

The Gospel of St John the Evangelist is recognized as the most mystical of the four Gospels, contemplating God directly in the same way as the eagle was said to look without flinching into the eye of the sun. The Evangelists appear in devotional art in the form of their symbols – a man, a lion and a bull representing Matthew, Mark and Luke respectively, along with an eagle for John. Church lecterns are often in the shape of a gilded eagle with wings outstretched, a powerful focus for the divine inspiration of Bible readings.

Both the eagle and the pelican are symbols of generosity. The eagle was believed to leave half its prey for other birds, even if it was still hungry; the pelican, according to legend, pecks at its breast to feed its young with its own blood, and so became seen in the Christian faith as symbolic of Jesus' sacrifice. A careful look around a medieval cathedral often reveals an endearing image, usually carved, of the 'Pelican in her Piety'.

lily and iris

Kempe's altarpiece in the Lady Chapel in Winchester Cathedral depicts the Annunciation. Dürer's study of a lily (above) is in the Monasterio de El Escorial, Spain.

Many flowers and plants have a hidden meaning and are often given as gifts to convey a special message – of love, for example, or friendship, remembrance or sympathy.

Although many flowers symbolize love and purity, and as such have a natural association with the Blessed Virgin, there are two that are regarded most particularly as her own – the lily and the iris. In representations of the Annunciation, the Archangel Gabriel holds a lily to signify the Immaculate Conception, and in images of the Virgin and Child the lily symbolizes chastity. Sometimes the lily is portrayed in the stylized form of an heraldic fleur-de-lis, which is also a symbol of the Holy Trinity.

The iris, or 'sword lily', is another symbol of the Immaculate Conception, and is also used to represent the Virgin's sorrow at the Passion of Christ.

St Joseph, too, has the attribute of a lily – in tradition, his staff sprouted to show that he was God's choice of a husband for Mary, and the blossoming staff became the lily to reflect the Virgin's attribute.

The lily is also a symbol of great beauty, and in Christian tradition this is translated into representing the beauty of the Church, an image inspired by the Song of Solomon:

'Like a lily among thorns is my darling among the maidens.'

Song of Solomon, 2:22

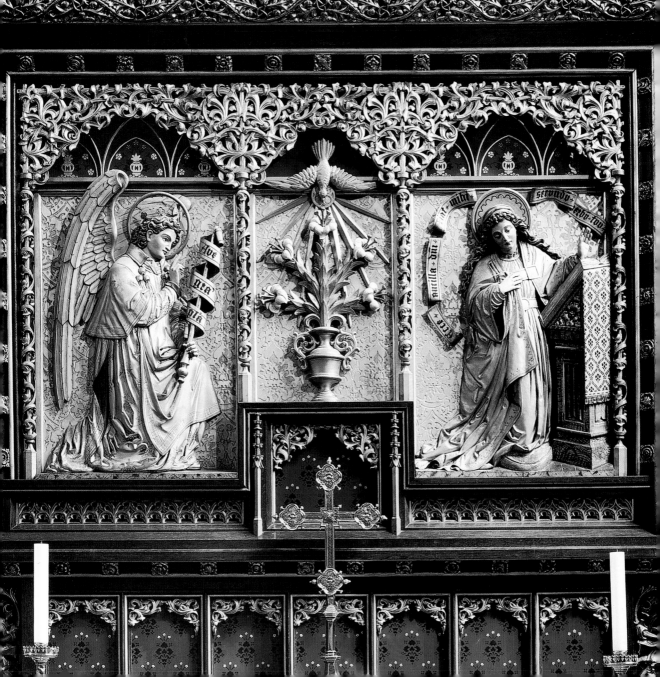

angels and archangels

Verrocchio's painting Tobias and the Angel, in The National Gallery, London. A detail from the Gate of Death memorial (right) in St Paul's Cathedral.

Angels are mystical beings that act as instruments of God – as counsellors, rulers and messengers. As beings of light, they have no real form or substance; thus, the portrayal of angels in a human form in devotional art is merely symbolic of their traditional associations.

The four archangels are messengers, and are led by St Michael. He is the protector of the Church, and is usually depicted as a great hero – young and handsome, he is dressed for battle and trampling Satan, often in the guise of a dragon. Sometimes Michael is shown holding scales to weigh the souls of the dead in Last Judgement scenes.

St Gabriel is best known for his role in appearing to the Virgin Mary at the Annunciation, and it is Gabriel who, traditionally, will blow the horn at the Last Judgement. Artistic portrayals of Gabriel show him as a powerful figure, richly robed, with large, colourful wings.

St Raphael, the guardian angel of all humanity, is depicted as a benign and mild figure, in humble pilgrim dress. He is protector of travellers, and also of the young and innocent; as such, Raphael is usually illustrated with the boy Tobias, from an apocryphal Old Testament story. Traditionally, it is St Raphael who, on Christmas night, brought the news of Christ's birth to the shepherds.

Uriel, the fourth of the archangels, is represented carrying a scroll and book to indicate his role as interpreter of judgements and prophecies.

numbers

The Holy Trinity by Botticelli, in the Courtauld Institute, London. The Seven Saints (above), by Fra Filippo Lippi,in The National Gallery, London, are believed to represent members of the influential Florentine Medici family.

Numbers are deeply symbolic in the Christian tradition. One, for example, is the symbol of unity, while thirteen, associated as it is with the Last Supper, denotes faithlessness and betrayal. Two represents the dual natures of Christ (human and divine), five symbolizes His wounds at the Crucifixion; eight, through the octagon that unifies God and earth, denotes the Resurrection. Six, the number of creation, symbolizes the qualities of divine power, majesty, wisdom, love, mercy and justice. Ten is the number of the Commandments; four is associated with the Evangelists, and twelve with Christ's Apostles.

The numbers three and seven, however, are the most sacred. Three is the divine number of the Trinity – Father, Son and Holy Ghost; Christ spent three days in the tomb before His Resurrection. The symbolic triangle of the Trinity is always equilateral – three equal parts joined as one; a triangular nimbus is used only in representations of God or the Trinity.

Seven is a powerful mystical number associated with perfection. God created the world in seven days; the seventh day, the Sabbath, is the day of rest. There are seven Sacraments (religious rites) including baptism, marriage and holy orders. The Seven Virtues (faith, hope, charity, temperance, prudence, fortitude and justice) offset the Seven Deadly Sins (pride, covetousness, lust, anger, gluttony, envy and sloth); the seven joys in the Virgin's life offset the seven sorrows she endured.

light

William Holman Hunt's The Light of the World *in St Paul's Cathedral.* Christ the Son of Man *(above), depicted by Charles Eamer Kempe in stained glass in Wakefield Cathdral.*

Light as the symbol of Christ stems from His words: 'I am the light of the world: whoever follows me will never walk in darkness, but will have the light of life' (John 8:12).

In sacred art, light is often depicted as an aureole, a glorious burst of golden radiance that seems to emanate from the figure it surrounds. As the symbol of divinity, its use is restricted to representations of the Father, the Son and the Holy Ghost, and of the Blessed Virgin. A halo of light around the head also defines the subject as sacred; its use is extended to less exalted figures, such as saints or donors.

The cross shown within a circular halo denotes redemption and portrays Christ as the Son of Man.

A famous representation of this symbol is *The Light of the World*, painted in 1854 by the Pre-Raphaelite artist William Holman Hunt. The figure of Christ emerges from the gloomy shadows of night, the golden halo around His head echoed in the warm, comforting glow of the lantern light; He is depicted knocking on a door with no handle, a symbolic reminder that God waits to enter the lives of those who invite him in.

THE   LIGHT
OF THE   WORLD

BEHOLD I STAND AT THE DOOR AND KNOCK IF ANY MAN
HEAR MY VOICE AND OPEN THE DOOR I WILL COME
IN TO HIM AND WILL SVP WITH HIM AND HE WITH ME.

water

Stephen Broadbent's statue The Water of Life *stands in the cloister garden of Chester Cathedral.*

Water is essential to life, and its practical necessity works hand-in-hand with its symbolic significance. Water not only represents cleansing and purifying, but is used for those purposes. It not only symbolizes new life, but new life cannot flourish without it. The use of water in baptism symbolizes the washing away of sin so that pure new life can emerge.

Stephen Broadbent's bronze statue *The Water of Life*, in the cloister garden of Chester Cathedral, depicts the story of Jesus and the Woman of Samaria. This story shows that, on a much deeper level, water also symbolizes faith; as water helps nurture the growth of a plant, so faith will sustain us through life and encourage us to blossom and grow.

The statue stands, appropriately, on the site of a well that supplied water to the medieval monks. The graceful, curving composition of the figures, almost meeting in a kiss above the bowl of water offered by Christ, evokes an image of life everlasting.

'... whoever drinks the water I give him will never thirst. Indeed, the water I give him will become in him a spring of water welling up to eternal life.'

Jesus and the Woman of Samaria, John 4:13–14

blue and gold

The right-hand section of the Wilton Diptych in The National Gallery, London. A golden sun (above) painted on the quire ceiling of Gloucester Cathedral. An icon (right) in Westminster Abbey, richly coloured in blue and gold.

Colours, too, have a meaning within the Christian faith; of these, the most joyful are the vibrant blues and golds that make sacred images so lustrous.

Blue is a deeply spiritual colour, the colour of the sky, linking it with heaven and divine love. The Virgin is usually, but not invariably, depicted in a blue gown, in shades from the deep blue of an almost-midnight sky to the fresh, pale blue of a rain-washed early morning. Blue is also associated with truth, for when the clouds of spiritual doubt and confusion clear from the mind, truth is revealed like a tiny patch of blue sky that slowly spreads.

Gold symbolizes the sun and divinity, the essence of Christ. It was adopted by the Renaissance painters to denote radiance, and the complex use of gold leaf in icons is a wonderful invitation to the human soul to be at one with the light of heaven.

'Praised be my Lord God ... for our brother the sun, who brings us the day and who brings us the light; fair is he and shines with a great splendour; O Lord, he signifies to us thee.'

St Francis of Assisi, Canticle of the Creatures

sacred materials

*T*he theme of God being present in all of Creation extends beyond the symbolism portrayed in devotional works of art to the materials used to create them. It may seem obvious that artistic materials were derived from

The Swansea altarpiece, a rare medieval carving in alabaster now in the Victoria and Albert Museum, London. Christ Crucified (above), a modern work by Peter Eugene Ball in Birmingham Cathedral.

the natural world – animal, vegetable and mineral - because, until recently, this was all that was available. But their use goes far beyond this practical consideration; they represent the union of heaven and earth, earthly materials to create a heavenly subject.

The earth itself was used to create one of the most ancient methods of focal contemplation in the form of a labyrinth. A long path twisting ever inward on itself until it reaches the centre, the labyrinth was etched into grass or formed with large pebbles; the

concept was almost certainly pagan, but was adopted, and adapted, by the Christian Church as it so perfectly represents the spiritual quest.

Once worship began to take place in churches, the earth's resources became part of the fabric of the buildings that were erected to the glory of God; and now that we are in the 21st century and recognizing just how precious are those resources, it is fitting that some of today's artists are making innovative use of recycled materials for their devotional works.

sculpture

A Romanesque carving in Chichester Cathedral depicting Christ being greeted at Bethany. The Last Supper (above), a detail from the high altar reredos in Liverpool Cathedral.

The natural world offers countless wonderful materials for sculpting – it yields up cool, smooth marble, rough stone and metals, translucent alabaster, wood from many different trees, plaster made from limestone, terracotta made from earth itself.

The term 'sculpture' covers any kind of three-dimensional representation, and is created using a variety of techniques including modelling and casting. For creating devotional pieces, carving is a deeply spiritual process –

not only is the material itself symbolic, but the creation involves the sculptor gradually whittling away whatever is not needed to reveal the figure, or figures, hidden at the heart of the raw material. A steady hand and a focused mind, as well as a certainty in knowing exactly when to stop, are essential. The beautiful depictions in cathedrals of the Crucifixion, as well as works such as screens and quire-stall decorations, demonstrate the depth of feeling and of expression that emerge from this 'subtractive' method of sculpting.

Oak is often used for carvings – it symbolizes strength, endurance, faith and virtue, and is one of the trees, along with the aspen and holly oak, from which the Cross is believed to have been created. Carvings, both in stone and wood, are sometimes gilded, touching the subject or scene with the light of heaven to magnificent effect.

manuscripts

Medieval monks created some marvellous devotional manuscripts, such as gospels and psalters, missals and hymnals. These books were decorated, or 'illuminated', so that the initial letters were almost lost in a burst of silver, gold and rich, brilliant colours that continued to follow their graceful trail around the margins.

The manuscripts were written on parchment or vellum, which was made from animal skins defleshed in a lime bath and whitened with chalk, using ink made of a mixture of gall and gum, coloured with carbon or with iron or copper salts. Paints were coloured with natural pigments, often with additions such as honey or eggshells to add texture and opacity. Real silver and gold, powdered down, were sometimes used to colour the ink, although gold leaf was also favoured as a rather less expensive alternative.

An exquisite example of a devotional manuscript is the rare 12th-century Winchester Bible, produced by one scribe and six illuminators on the skins of more than 250 calves. Gold leaf gleams from its precious pages, and the intense blue was created from crushed lapis lazuli, a costly semi-precious stone flecked with gold that was much used in medieval art. Its dazzling depth is reminiscent of the heavens.

Illuminated initial letters from the 12th-century Winchester Bible. An illuminated letter from the Romsey Psalter, c.1440, in Romsey Abbey (above). An illustration from the 14th-century Litlyngton Missal in Westminster Abbey (right).

Sed in lege dñi uoluntas ei · & in lege eius medita   Sed in lege dñi uoluntas eiuf · & in lege

paintings

The Christ Child dictates the Magnificat to the Virgin in this painting by Botticelli, in the Galleria degli Uffizi, Florence, Italy. The Virgin with the Child Jesus, St Anne and St John the Baptist (above), a cartoon by Leonardo da Vinci in The National Gallery, London.

A Renaissance painting began with a drawing, often in charcoal and chalk, known as a 'cartoon'; this image was transferred to the picture surface by pricking the outline with a pin and then dusting the pinholes with soot. In the Early Renaissance period, pictures were usually painted on a soft wood, such as poplar or lime, as it was slightly absorbent and made a good base for tempera paint.

Tempera is known to be one of the oldest mediums for painting, and is made by adding finely ground dry pigments to pure egg yolk. The egg is the symbol of hope and resurrection, so tempera is very appropriate for use in devotional paintings – indeed, it is still favoured by the Orthodox Church. The white of the egg made the paint dry very rapidly, and also dragged when it was applied to the wood, so it was carefully excluded.

By the 16th century, tempera had given way to oil paint, the pigments being added to an oil that dried, usually linseed, which also had the advantage of safely sealing the picture. Sometimes, tempera and oil paints were used together; adding details in oil paint added some texture to the flat tempera, enabling High Renaissance artists to indulge their new delight in depicting light, shade and depth.

frescoes

The Creation of the Sun (right) and God Dividing Light from Darkness (above), details from Michelangelo's fresco on the ceiling of the Sistine Chapel in Rome, Italy.

A fresco, or mural, is painted onto the walls of a cathedral or church, and thus it becomes part of the fabric of the building. It is the work of a visionary – every detail is planned in advance, and precise allowance must be made for the colours fading deep into the plaster.

Colour pigments are ground to a fine powder with a pestle and mortar before they are added to the water-based paint medium. The artist works on freshly applied, perfectly smooth, damp plaster made of a mixture of powdered marble and limestone; as it dries and hardens, a chemical reaction between the plaster and the natural carbon dioxide in the air holds the pigment in a hard crust of calcium carbonate.

If the work is touched up after the plaster has dried, then it cannot, strictly speaking, be called a true fresco; thus the plaster is applied in sections and painted before it hardens. Speed is of the essence, as the outline of the design must be transferred to the damp plaster before painting begins.

The Renaissance was without doubt the golden age of the true fresco, and Michelangelo's painting on the ceiling of the Sistine Chapel is the outstanding example of this skilful art form. It is quite remarkable that the artist carried out part of the work while lying flat on his back on a platform.

icons

An icon of the Holy Trinity by Andrei Rublev c.1370–1430, in Moscow's Tretyakov Gallery in Russia. An icon (above) in St Davids Cathedral depicting Elijah being fed by the ravens.

In the Russian Orthodox tradition, an icon can only be created by someone who is wholly comfortable with his or her spiritual nature, for it is necessary to allow the ego to dissolve and let the intuition of the soul shine through to be captured in the image.

Any holy figure can be chosen as the subject – Christ giving a blessing, the Madonna and Child, angels or saints, events in the lives of the Holy Family, whatever resonates with the painter.

Building the icon is a highly complex business. It is painted on wood, which is first prepared with several layers of gesso (white plaster); this is sanded to a smooth finish to take the drawn image. Next, precious gold leaf is laid down and burnished; this represents the holy light of heaven. Finally the colours are applied, wonderful earthy pigments such as ochre, umber and terre-verte. These are layered up, starting with the deepest colour and finishing with the palest, reflecting the human spiritual journey from darkness to light. Finally, highlights are added and the icon is named and blessed.

In the creation of an icon, there are two vital elements that portray the mystery of the Christian faith and urge the worshipper to look deep within for the truth – thus, it is impossible to catch the eye of the subject, and the mouth is always very firmly closed.

fabrics

A detail of the processional banner in York Minster. An ecclesiastical cushion (above) designed by Pugin, in the Victoria and Albert Museum, London. A detail (right) of a 14th-century cope in the Glastonbury Abbey museum.

Natural fabrics are ideal for devotional art as they are organic – cotton, wool and especially wild silk. This precious material is made by a 'silkworm', the caterpillar of the *Bombyx mori* moth, which spins a cocoon of silk before it changes into its pupal state. Butterflies and moths are symbolic of the Resurrection both of Christ and of mankind – the three stages of their existence, as caterpillar, chrysalis and butterfly/moth, are perfect analogies for life, death and resurrection.

Gold-threadwork was traditionally used for ecclesiastical purposes, and was a very highly valued skill in medieval times, when vestments and wall-hangings were richly decorated with figures embroidered in metal and silk threads and embellished with enamel, pearls, precious stones, paste diamonds and coral. Embroidery with gold thread produces a quite spectacular effect – flat embroidery lends the impression of fabric woven with gold, while laying out a design in fine cord and over-sewing it with metal thread produces an image in relief.

York Minster's wonderfully rich and tactile processional banner, dating from the early years of the First World War, is a stunning modern example. Made from luxurious velvet and silk, with shimmering gold-thread embroidery, the work is laid against a sumptuous background of rose-red silk damask.

stained glass

A Kempe window in Wells Cathedral. A late 12th-century window in Canterbury Cathedral (above left). A detail (above right) of a 17th-century window in University College Chapel, Oxford.

The miraculous transformation of an unpromising substance like sand into transparent glass is in itself a process laden with symbolism. Coloured and painted, glass has been a wonderful medium for ecclesiastical artistry since the mid 12th century.

The earliest stained-glass technique involved adding metallic oxides to the molten glass to colour it – cobalt for blue, copper for green, iron for red, and so on. A thin layer of the coloured glass was then applied to white glass. The sheets of glass were nibbled into shape to fit the design and the details – faces, folds in the drapery, inscriptions – were added in black paint. Finally, the design was assembled and bound with strips of grooved lead.

The weighty, primitive effect of this 'pot-metal' method became lighter with technical developments, changing tastes and architectural advancement.

Windows became smaller, needing less lead, and more white glass was used to let in light. From the mid 16th century enamel was used to paint the glass, producing very delicate images. The Victorians, with their love of Gothic, returned to the pot-metal method; the stained-glass maker Charles Eamer Kempe, who made a study of medieval glass, evolved a style that combined the best of all worlds, softening rich green, blue and ruby glass with large areas of ethereal silver stain.

recycling for the modern age

Helen Jennings'
sculpture Christ
Crucified *in Coventry*
Cathedral. Peter Eugene
Ball's sculpture Christ
in Majesty *(above) in*
Ely Cathedral.

Recycled materials are an innovative way to create devotional sculptures that both respect the need to preserve the earth's natural resources and symbolize the transformation of something that has been discarded or damaged into an object of power and beauty.

Peter Eugene Ball takes pieces of driftwood found on the seashore, oak beams from demolished houses, even redundant railway sleepers and then applies brass, copper, gold leaf and earthy paint colours to create a *pietà*, a Crucifixion, a Christ in Majesty that is naive, almost folk-arty in style and yet moving in its very simplicity. Ball is particularly drawn to driftwood as a medium, as any soft wood is worn away by the sea to leave the natural shape of the hard wood, complete with defects that become a part of the work. His fascination with both Romanesque and Celtic style and with ancient neolithic monuments is reflected in the faces of his figures and the swirling decoration of their robes.

Another innovative modern sculptor, Helen Jennings, used the wreckage of a crashed car to create her powerful and thought-provoking *Christ Crucified* for Coventry Cathedral. The city is at the heart of England's car-manufacturing business, and this stark reminder of the pain inflicted on man by man through careless driving is a sobering theme.

the human element

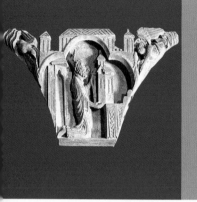

*S*acred art is very much about the divine characters in the Christian story and the signs and symbols that represent them. It is a remarkably powerful visual lesson in the teachings of Christ and an inspiration to the

human soul, to be visited and revisited as often as wished. To some, the scenes depicted are so familiar that they need only act as a gentle reminder, especially in troubled times; for others, they can create the stirrings of a desire to look more deeply within themselves and make that spiritual connection.

Churches and cathedrals are built to the glory of God, and in so doing mankind acknowledges God's unfailing efforts to bring about its salvation. Anyone who has ever been involved in physically constructing a church or in

spiritually supporting the Church – anyone who believes that goodness overcomes evil, and darkness gives way to light – has, in so doing, left behind a little bit of his or her soul to help the spiritual progress of others. Their contribution is valuable in its own right, and almost as much a work of devotional art as the most treasured painting or sculpture.

So this is where we part company with the Divine and take a look at the human element – which, of course, invariably leads back to the Divine.

wanted: stonemason with g.s.o.h.

The agonies of toothache portrayed in a capital in Wells Cathedral (right) and of seasickness on a misericord in St Davids Cathedral (above). Another capital in Wells (below right) shows a man and boy stealing fruit.

A careful scrutiny of any church or cathedral will reveal that those who spent weeks, months, years taking part in its creation appeared to do so in a spirit of pure joy. Yes, all the essential ingredients are there to guide the worshipper on the symbolic journey along the Christian path as he or she progresses through the building – powerful images of the life of Christ and the Holy Family, of pious saints and wretched martyrs; but look in the less obvious places and you'll see evidence of life as it is lived every day.

One might be forgiven for imagining that a medieval advertisement to recruit builders would run along the lines of, say: 'Stonemasons and woodcarvers wanted – experience preferred (although training will be given); good sense of humour essential.'

For humour is everywhere – in the stone carvings, in the roof bosses, in the misericords; these craftsmen took delight in their work and wanted to be remembered for it. So they appear with all their human ailments and foibles – clutching an aching tooth or stomach, stealing the odd thing here and there, getting into a fight – an endearing reminder that the world around might change, but the nature of man stays the same and the circle of life just keeps on turning.

everything changes ...

Antony Gormley's sculpture Sound II *in the crypt of Winchester Cathedral. The cathedral's statue of the Madonna and Child (above) survived the post-Dissolution iconoclasm, but not completely intact.*

... *but God changes not.*

One of the most comforting things about going into a very old cathedral or church is the feeling of peace and stability that hangs in the air, the feeling that it has survived through centuries of conflict and change. When there is turmoil all around, it is good to stand very still, breathe deeply and quietly absorb that indescribable sense of continuity. But it's also good to remember that some of those buildings have struggled to survive, and in this way reflect the human condition.

Winchester Cathedral is a splendid example; this plucky medieval church withstood the attacks of iconoclasts following Henry VIII's Dissolution of the Monasteries and during the Civil War, only to succumb – very nearly – to severe subsidence caused by seasonal flooding in the crypt. Its rescue, carried out during the early 20th century by a deep-sea diver who underpinned the medieval walls with huge quantities of concrete, is legendary.

The crypt continues to flood in winter, but the danger has passed. Antony Gormley's serenely beautiful sculpture, *Sound II*, stands in the crypt's north aisle; the flood-water is drawn up through the body and spills out from the cupped hands of the solitary figure, caught in perpetual contemplation of the rivers of chaos that humanity has tried so hard to contain.

'Lord of all gentleness,
Lord of all calm,
Whose voice is contentment,
whose presence is balm ...'

Jan Struther, 1901–53

sacred stitches

Details of The Banner of Our Lady, *made by a parishioner of Exeter Cathedral; the* Energy *altar frontal (above) in Salisbury Cathedral, made by the Sarum Group of the Embroiderers' Guild; and a cushion (right), made by the Embroidery Guild of St Davids Cathedral for the Dean's stall.*

Perhaps the most unsung heroes and heroines among sacred artists are those patient and devoted craftspeople whose contribution lies not in their use of the quill pen, the paintbrush or the sculpting tool, but in their sure and deft skill with a sewing needle.

Fabric, as we have seen, is perfect for creating devotional images and in the right hands can be transformed into majestic ceremonial banners, evocative altar cloths, and even plump kneelers to spare the discomfort of worshippers kneeling at prayer. These kneelers spend much of their time tucked away out of sight, yet as much thought and care has gone into their creation as into that of an intricate wall-hanging; they are often made in commemoration of an important anniversary or event in the history of the church or its environs.

Most works of sacred art are created by an individual working in splendid isolation, the communion flowing directly between the artist and God; but the 'soft furnishings' that go into a church or cathedral are often made by local parishioners or the members of an embroidery guild working together, bringing in a new and very important layer to the creative process – a sense of communion with each other.

prisoners of conscience

Details from lancets in the Prisoners of Conscience window in Salisbury Cathedral.

The startling Prisoners of Conscience window in the Trinity Chapel at the east end of Salisbury Cathedral is magnificent, and a worthy offering to greet the rising sun. The predominant colour used in the window is a rich, very intense blue, which echoes the heavenly skies and makes a fitting end to the symbolic spiritual journey that we follow through the cathedral.

This fine window was designed by a renowned contemporary stained-glass maker from France, Gabriel Loire, and installed in 1980 in five of the cathedral's original lancets. The centre three show the Crucifixion with Jesus as a 1st-century prisoner of conscience, while in the outer two the theme has been sensitively echoed with depictions of some of the prisoners of conscience who took a stand against the atrocities of the 20th century. The detail in the expressions on the faces is quite extraordinary, ranging from fear and bewilderment to total confidence and understanding.

What makes this window so special is that the prisoners represented are themselves a human manifestation of devotional art, expressing the profound truth taught by all spiritual traditions – that we are all one, and therefore when we harm each other we are harming ourselves. It is sometimes believed that prisoners of conscience act out of fear or cowardice, when usually they are doing the opposite by standing up for firmly held beliefs that love and harmony, not hate and tyranny, are the fundamental truths.

reconciliation

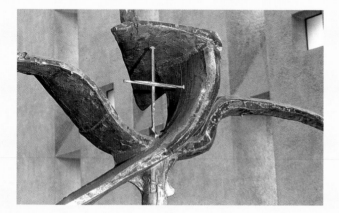

The Reconciliation *statue in the ruins of Coventry Cathedral. The Cross of Nails (above) was made from nails found in the debris of the medieval cathedral.*

The loss of life and the devastation presented an enormous challenge in forgiveness to all those affected – one that was met with grace and a generous recognition that all sides in the war had suffered. A new cathedral was built alongside the ruins of the old, which are preserved as a focus of prayer for reconciliation and world peace.

The new cathedral is filled with images reflecting this theme; one of the most inspiring and deeply moving is the statue *Reconciliation* by Josefina de Vasconcellos, created by the sculptor when she was 90 years old. Standing at the point where the new cathedral joins the ruins, it depicts two human figures locked in a heartfelt embrace; there are versions in the Hiroshima Peace Park in Japan, at the site of the Berlin Wall in Germany and in the grounds of Stormont Castle in Belfast, Northern Ireland.

While in an ideal world there would be no wars, we are, at present, a very long way from such a world; however, any conflict, from a minor skirmish to a major battle, offers opportunities for us to learn about the importance of forgiveness and reconciliation.

This lesson has been embraced wholeheartedly in Coventry, where the old medieval cathedral was all but destroyed in a German bombing raid on the night of 14 November 1940.

THE GIRDLERS CHAPEL

'Reconciliation'

In 1995,50 years after the end of the Second World War this sculpture
by Josefina de Vasconcellos has been given by Richard Branson as a
token of reconciliation.

An identical sculpture has been placed on behalf of the people of
Coventry in the Peace Garden, Hiroshima, Japan.

Both sculptures remind us that, in the face of destructive forces,human
dignity and love will triumph over disaster and bring nations together in
respect and peace.

ジョセフィナ・デ・ヴァスコンチェロス女史制作のこの彫像は、
第2次世界大戦終結から50年を経過した1995年、平和の証しとして、
日本の広島市在住のリチャード・ブランソン氏より寄贈さ
れたものです。

また、本像と同一の彫像が、コベントリー市民に代わり、日本
の広島市の平和公園にも据えられました。

この2つの像は私達に次のように思い起こさせてくれます。

────人類の尊厳と愛は、いかなる破壊力にも勝ることにより(尊
厳を支援し、諸国民を平和のうちに結束と親睦を結ぶ。────

divine love

The expression 'the fear of God' is one that is often used; yet throughout the centuries those who have recorded their personal encounters with the Divine invariably speak not of a power to be feared, but of one that radiates love.

One of the most famous English mystics was a recluse, Dame Julian of Norwich (*c*.1342–*c*.1416), who lived out a solitary existence in a tiny cell adjoining a church in the city, spending her time in prayer and contemplation but also helping those who sought her advice. She took to this way of life after a series of visions of Christ's Passion came to her and brought about her recovery from illness when she was on the point of death.

Dame Julian's account of the visions, entitled 'Revelations of Divine Love', emphasizes the power of the love of God, and is a work that continues to influence theologians to this day.

The familiar and inspiring words associated with Julian are infinitely comforting in times of sadness and difficulty, or when we simply seek a little spiritual reassurance:

'All shall be well, and all shall be well, and all manner of thing shall be well.'

A statue of Dame Julian of Norwich in a niche on the West Front of Norwich Cathedral. The stained-glass window (left) is in the city's Church of St Julian.

77

bibliography/further information

ART HISTORY: A VERY SHORT
INTRODUCTION
Dana Arnold (Oxford University Press,
Oxford, 2004)

BOTTICELLI
Barbara Deimling (Taschen, Cologne, 2000)

DÜRER AND THE VIRGIN IN THE
GARDEN
Susan Foister (National Gallery Company Ltd,
London, 2004)

HOW TO READ A CHURCH
Richard Taylor (Rider/Ebury Press, London,
2003, 2004 [illustrated])

ITALIAN RENAISSANCE PAINTING
Sara Elliott (Phaidon Press Ltd, London,
1993)

MICHELANGELO
Gilles Néret (Taschen, Cologne, 2000)

SIGNS AND SYMBOLS IN CHRISTIAN ART
George Ferguson (Oxford University Press,
New York, 1954)

The examples in this book of sacred art in
UK cathedrals/abbeys are in the following
locations: Birmingham (West Midlands);
Canterbury (Kent); Carlisle (Cumbria); Chester
(Cheshire); Chichester (West Sussex); Coventry
(Warwickshire); Ely (Cambridgeshire); Exeter
(Devon); Glastonbury (Somerset); Gloucester
(Gloucestershire); Lichfield (Staffordshire); Liverpool
(Merseyside); Norwich (Norfolk); Oxford
(Oxfordshire); Portsmouth (Hampshire); Rochester
(Kent); Romsey (Hampshire); St Albans
(Hertfordshire); St Davids (Pembrokeshire); St Paul's
(London); Salisbury (Wiltshire); Wakefield (West
Yorkshire); Wells (Somerset); Westminster Abbey
(London); Winchester (Hampshire); Worcester
(Worcestershire); York (Yorkshire).

THE NATIONAL GALLERY, LONDON, has
an excellent 'Life of Christ' trail.

index

acknowledgements

Photographs are reproduced by kind permission of the following:
Bridgeman Art Library: pp10 (Hermitage, St Petersburg, Russia), 11, 13 (both National Gallery, London), 14 (Santa Maria delle Grazie, Italy), 15 (St Peter's, Vatican City, Italy), 16, 17 (both National Gallery, London), 18 (Graphische Sammlung Albertina, Vienna, Austria), 19 (Hermitage, St Petersburg, Russia), 22 (Arts Council Collection, Hayward Gallery, London), 34 (Monasterio de El Escorial, El Escorial, Spain), 39 (Courtauld Institute Galleries, London), 45, 52 (both National Gallery, London), 53 (Galleria degli Uffizi, Florence, Italy), 54, 55 (both Vatican Museums and Galleries, Vatican City, Italy), 57 (Tretyakov Gallery, Moscow), end papers (Virgin and Child); Alistair Carew-Cox: pp46 (courtesy of the Dean and Chapter of Birmingham Cathedral), 75 (courtesy of Coventry Cathedral); Christie's Images: p20; Collections: pp28, 36; John Crook: pp30, 32 left, 35, 49, 51, 68, 69; Fogg Art Museum, Harvard University Art Museums, Bequest of Grenville L. Winthrop: p21; Trustees of Glastonbury Abbey: p58 right; Sonia Halliday Photographs: front cover, pp1, 3, 9, 60 left, 60 right, 72, 73; Robert Hupka: p14; Chapter of Lichfield Cathedral: p29; National Gallery, London: pp7, 26, 27, 37, 38; National Gallery of Art, Washington: p12; St Davids Cathedral: pp31 (by C.R.A. Davies), 56, 66 left (both by Pitkin Publishing), 70 right (by C.R.A. Davies); St Paul's Cathedral: p40; Pitkin Publishing: pp6, 8, 25, 32 right, 33, 42, 43, 44 left, 48, 62, 63, 65, 66 left, 66 right, 67, 70 left, 71, 74, 76, end papers (Christ Crucified); Portsmouth Cathedral: p24; Rector and P.C.C. of St John the Baptist Timberhill with St Julian's: p77; Tate Picture Library: p23; Victoria and Albert Museum: pp47, 58 left; Dean and Chapter of Wakefield: p40; Wells Cathedral (by the late Richard Neale): 61; Dean and Chapter of Westminster: pp44 right, 50 bottom; Ian Whatmore (courtesy of Romsey Abbey): p50 top; Dean and Chapter of York: p59.

All efforts were made to trace copyright holders. The publishers will be pleased to rectify any omissions in future editions.